BRITISH
TIPPER LORRIES

BILL REID

AMBERLEY

Acknowledgements

I would like to thank Ian Lawson, Pat Crang, Paul Heanachon, Alex Syme, Eddie Waugh, Brian McGinlay and Bob Matthews for allowing me to use their photos in the compilation of this book.

Many of the photos used are my own or have come from my collection, with no known copyright, and I would like to thank anybody who recognises their photos for having the foresight to take it, in the furtherance of road transport enthusiasm.

First published 2019

Amberley Publishing
The Hill, Stroud
Gloucestershire, GL5 4EP

www.amberley-books.com

Copyright © Bill Reid, 2019

The right of Bill Reid to be identified as the Author of this work has been asserted in accordance with the Copyright, Designs and Patents Act 1988.

ISBN 978 1 4456 7296 0 (print)
ISBN 978 1 4456 7297 7 (ebook)

British Library Cataloguing in Publication Data. A catalogue record for this book is available from the British Library.

Origination by Amberley Publishing.
Printed in the UK.

Introduction

The origin of tipper lorries lies in days of horse-drawn transport, well before the coming of motorised transport. There has always been a need to transport goods and people overland and many different types of wagons and carts were used with varying amounts of real horsepower. Just as the motor bus developed from the stagecoach, load-carrying motor lorries evolved from horse-drawn equipment.

Tipping horse-drawn carts were a means for the hauling and disposal of bulk commodities, albeit in small quantities. The body of the carts were centrally pivoted to allow them to tip rearward, using the force of gravity and some judicious loading. With the arrival of motorised transport the same principle applied until loads became heavier and could not be tipped by hand.

The means of tipping the heavier loads initially was by manpower and screw jacks. Winding handles turned a long screw fitted to the front of the body and by some hard work the load could be tipped out. In time, hydraulic pressure was harnessed by way of a gearbox power take-off pump and telescopic rams to elevate the body and tip the load.

In the beginning tipper lorries were small, based on the lorry manufacturers' products of the time. As a consequence they did not carry much more than the horse-drawn tipping carts, sometimes known as box carts, or tumbrils, but were much faster than a carthorse. Also, the lorries did not need the same attention as a working horse.

By the 1920s lorries were becoming larger and stronger, capable of carrying heavier payloads. About this time, three-axle lorries were developing, again raising the payload capability. Different types of tipping bodies had appeared, particularly those that could tip to the side, a boon in some trades like road building. Pneumatic tyres were being fitted, making for a smoother ride, although this was not essential in tipper haulage, and having less of an impact on road surfaces.

In the 1930s four-axle lorries began to appear in all forms of goods transport. Tipper versions were offered by all the heavy lorry manufacturers due to their increased capacity. Back then, there were no plating regulations, although the law set the gross weight at 12 tons for a two-axle lorry, 19 tons for a three-axle lorry, and 22 tons for a four-axle type. However, overloading was an everyday occurrence, and many lorries ran in excess of the legal weights.

Various types of lorry evolved in the 1930s and into the Second World War years. A version of the three-axle lorry was the twin steer, with two steering axles and a single rear axle. This set-up produced a lighter lorry with the expectation of a higher load capacity. Similarly, third-axle conversions were popular on lighter lorries to increase the payload potential within the basic gross weight limits.

Every type of lorry put on sale in Britain was utilised as a tipper, some in short wheelbase lengths, others much longer. No specific make was built as a tipper, and each manufacturer was able to provide chassis and wheelbases to suit the individual buyer. Manufacturers like Bedford and Ford were able to supply a complete tipper from the production line, if specified. Many engineering companies provided bespoke bodies and tipping gear for fitting to new chassis and cabs, Bromilow & Edwards (later to be named Edbro) and Telehoist, to name but two.

Tipping bodies were made of wood, perhaps with a steel floor to counteract the impact of loads, often with dropsides, with a move to all-steel or aluminium construction. Aluminium was used when the loads were less coarse and, being lighter than steel, afforded a little more payload. Insulated bodies for the haulage of tarmacadam became common, virtually ending the wooden-sided types.

There had been small increases in gross weights for three- and four-axle types in the 1950s, but a much larger increase in 1964 to 32 tons gross for articulated lorries saw a big change in tipper use, allowing much larger lorries and loads. The traditional four-axle tippers were at a disadvantage because of restrictive axle spacing rules, which went against their use. The three-axle type was a better proposition and saw an increase in sales at the time.

Subsequent changes in legal gross weights allowed four-axle lorries to run at 32 tons gross weight, with better axle spacing. The eight-wheeler tipper has dominated the tipper trade for a long time, with its inherent stability and reasonable payload. Articulated lorries had an upgrade to 38 tons gross weight, then 44 tons, which made them capable of 24- or 25-ton loads. Much use is made of articulated tippers in long-distance bulk haulage, with the eight-wheelers more commonly used in local circumstances.

There are many types of tipping lorries, from the traditional style for fast loading and tipping, carrying any commodity that can be lifted and tipped, and container trailers that can be tipped to empty the carried container, to bulk powder tankers and waste disposal types.

With the coming of larger trailers, there is a danger of this type tipping over sideways, to the detriment of life and severe damage to the vehicle. Walking floor trailers, where the load is ejected without the body being lifted, are now common and should be considered as tippers, in my opinion. Generally, this method of unloading has been instigated by health and safety requirements, along with the need for tipper loads to be covered.

Tipper lorries have had a bad reputation for being dirty, noisy and badly maintained vehicles, with insecure loads and drivers who have little regard for other road users.

Hopefully, with operator licensing obligations and driver certification that impression will be a conception of the past. The present-day tipper generally gives a much better public impression, with well-designed cabs and equipment and drivers trained to above acceptable standards.

Where it all began: a horse with a tip or box cart. These carts were built by local agricultural engineers and varied in style from district to district. The box was pivoted at the end of the shafts and tipping was by gravity and fine balance of the load.

Robert Wynn was a large user of horses and carts and this picture shows one of their outfits being loaded with an early mechanical digger. The horseman is holding the horse's bridle, reassuring it against the noise of the machine. This cart has been fitted with heavy lorry wheels.

An Albion A10 3-tonner, lettered for Kilmarnock District Committee, in Ayrshire when brand new and unregistered, around 1910. It is demonstrating the ability to side tip, which would be useful to a local authority maintaining narrow roads.

Leyland lorries of the early 1920s were still looking much like the wartime RAF type. This is a PH2 5-tonner, in preservation, and close inspection reveals a heavy, rugged lorry. It has a basic wooden braced tipper body of about 6 cubic yards' capacity.

Another lorry in preservation is this 30 cwt (1.5-ton) Ford BB. It appears to have screw jack lifting gear, with the winding spindle behind the cab step, like that for semi-trailer legs.

A Leyland Hippo lorry with a registration dating from 1931 being loaded rather optimistically by three men with shovels. Is it a posed shot? It is a three-way tipper, in that it can be arranged to tip to either side or to the rear.

Tippers were by no means confined to petrol or diesel lorries, as this steam-driven Sentinel in preservation shows. It has been posed with a period face shovel, which might also be steam-driven.

The majority of lorries were manufactured by mass production, and were generally lightweights against the likes of Foden, AEC and ERF. This somewhat anonymous Fordson 7V was used by London Transport in its Buildings Department. Fitted with a V8 engine and a clanging steel body, it would no doubt herald its arrival.

The Royal Burgh of Ayr, the county town of Ayrshire, used this Scammell Mechanical Horse as a refuse collector with a dual-purpose trailer, which could tip refuse to the rear and store salvaged material in the front compartment. This was an unusual type in Scotland.

Two Foden DG eight-wheel lorries, with the left-hand one carrying a 1933 registration. Both are three-way tippers on very short wheelbases, with a gross legal weight of 22 tons. The streamlined cab design was not liked by drivers as it created a blind spot above the front side windows. It was later changed to a more square-shaped style.

A line of seven Dennis Pax 5-tonners supplied new to the British Quarrying Co. Ltd, all fitted with front end hydraulic tipping gear. Dennis lorries have been well favoured by local authorities over the years, up to the present day.

A wartime Austin K4 posing outside the premises of Bromilow & Edwards, who would have supplied the tipping gear and perhaps the dropside body. The Austin chassis on a long wheelbase provided plenty of body length. The underfloor tipping ram would allow the body to be close to the cab, suggesting that the lorry was also used for general haulage.

A new-looking wartime Bedford OWL, but carrying a 1948 registration, suggesting it is an ex-military lorry rebuilt with commercial wheels and tyres. It carries a tipper body built in the traditional wooden style and no doubt was a cheaper alternative to a new lorry.

The Maudslay Motor Co. became a constituent of AEC, and lorry production stopped in favour of AEC types. This is a late Mogul, their name for four-wheelers, ready for delivery to a Halifax company. Dual underfloor hydraulic rams lift the tipping body. A typical 12-ton gross lorry of the time – compare it with a modern 12-tonner.

Due to the scarcity of new lorries after the Second World War, many adaptions were made to keep haulage operators running. This is a former wartime military Leyland Hippo that has been fitted with an additional steering axle to uprate its load capacity. It would have been an ideal lorry for heavy muck shifting work. The military slinging points are still fitted to the hubs.

Proctor of Norwich was one of a number of new lorry builders in the late 1940s, using a Perkins engine and proprietary running gear. A 5- to 6-ton tipper is shown here, with underfloor tipping gear and a wooden body. Proctors were only made for a few years.

The Albion heavyweight range was known as the CX. Four, six and eight-wheelers were available, with four- or six-cylinder engines. The CX range was always identifiable by the headlamp mountings beside the radiator.

Another Austin from the Bromilow & Edwards publicity file, showing a new three-way tipper for John Mowlem & Co. Ltd. This is a 5-ton K4, which was sometimes referred to as the Birmingham Bedford, due to their similarity. Bromilow & Edwards would later become known as Edbro.

The Albion CX was a well-favoured heavy lorry in the bulk tipper trade and this well-used example, dating from 1950, has a heavy duty appearance with oversize front tyres and a strongly built steel dropside body.

In the immediate post-war years, new lorries were difficult to obtain and rebuilds were common. This preserved example of a wartime Bedford OWL, with the utility front, was typical and was virtually identical to the later Bedford OAL when it became available.

Horace Kendrick was a large Midlands tipper operator with a fleet dominated by Fodens. This time-served Foden FG has been converted from a tipper to be the fleet recovery truck, with the recovery gear fitted within the old tipper body.

A 1947 Seddon Mk 5S in the former Glasgow fleet of James Hemphill. Seddon diesel lorries were built in Oldham with Perkins engines and were popular for local haulage. The Mk 5 type was one of the longer running Seddon models, and was still available in the 1960s.

Albion introduced a new heavyweight range known as the HD in 1950, using their own six-cylinder engines. By 1952, when this tipper was new, it might have been fitted with the Leyland O.600 engine. This is a posed picture showing the body stabiliser.

Another posed picture, this time from the ERF publicity department, of two ERF 68G tippers about to enter the BRS fleet in 1951. BRS tippers ran in a light grey livery, distinguishing them from the massive red general haulage fleet.

The tipper lorry that was made famous, or notorious, by the film *Hell Drivers*. The Dodge Kew was a substantial bonneted type rated up to 7 tons, using Perkins engines. It is said that Drinkwater tippers were used in the making of *Hell Drivers*.

Albions were seen as rugged, economical lorries with a basic long-lasting specification. This FT3 model was used by the Burgh of Hawick as a refuse collector, with an end-tipping kerbside collection body, sometimes known as a fish fryer style.

The Austin Loadstar was the successor to the K types and had a larger cab that was styled on contemporary Austin cars. This end-tipper with a wooden body would deliver about 5 cubic yards of material.

The Bedford OST was in competition with the Austin Loadstar, but was by far the more common type. This one, for Glasgow Corporation, fitted out as a three-way tipper, is seen brand new and unregistered.

Shelvoke & Drewry (SD) were well known for building municipal vehicles. This restored 1950s Freighter represents a refuse collector used by the former Royal Burgh of Maybole. It was rebuilt by the owner, Mick Cooper, and has the typical side-loading end-tipper body of its time.

At a time when most lorry mass producers had forward and normal control types, this Morris Commercial LC 3-tonner was relatively rare among its contemporaries. A side valve petrol engine may not have enhanced its popularity. This is a rare example in preservation.

Dennis Brothers were well known for their municipal vehicles and this Stroud Council three-way tipper was probably part of a fleet of Dennis lorries. It is a Pax, so named for Peace, after the end of the Second World War, with a sizeable body in typical off-road operating conditions.

A Morris FE 5-tonner in the new BMC range of lorries. They were available badged as Austin or Morris, with petrol or diesel engines. The 4-litre, six-cylinder petrol engine was the same as that used in the Princess limousines. Note the tailboard release handle on the front of the steel body.

Foden was a builder of eight-wheeler lorries from the 1930s and their eight-wheelers were always popular. This FG with a Foden S20 cab displaying underfloor tipping gear, fitted to the outside of the chassis frame, could be specified with a Foden two-stroke engine or a conventional Gardner diesel.

The semi-forward control Leyland Comet was the first new design of Leyland lorry in the post-war years. It used a cab structure similar to Ford and Dodge, and was rated initially as a 7-tonner. Blue Circle had a large fleet of Comets, which were made well known by the Dinky Toy model. This is an ultra-short tanker that tipped for unloading.

Bedford produced a medium weight lorry in the 1940s and 1950s known as the M Type. It had normal control, with a longer bonnet than the OAL, and found use with small companies and local authorities, as seen here, tipping salvaged material.

Thornycroft built lorries that were considered a cut above the mass-produced types, and as such they were not seen in great quantities. The National Coal Board used this one, dating from 1954, in the then extensive Ayrshire coalfield. It is a Sturdy, with a proprietary Motor Panels cab, used on various other Thornycroft and Guy lorries.

The Bedford OST short wheelbase tipper is well remembered and respected, judging by the number in preservation. A Bedford salesman's handbook of 1948 shows that the cost of a complete tipper such as this, fully built by the Bedford factory, would have been £596!

The Co-operative Wholesale Society had various uses for heavy tippers, and this AEC Mammoth Major Mk III carries a large bulk flour body, which would be tipped for discharge of the load. It has the so-called 'tin front' cab, as a modernisation feature.

Richard Biffa is a long-established waste materials haulier and is still a name in present-day waste disposal. This 1957-registered Foden FG, on a very short wheelbase and with a high-sided body, would be instrumental in moving London's rubbish out of the city.

As the 1950s progressed Bedford replaced the O Type lorry with the A Type, featuring an American-style cab similar to Chevrolet trucks. This one is seen outside a Scottish Bedford dealer's premises, awaiting delivery to Robert Paterson, a company still in business supplying the building industry.

As rugged a tipper as you can get, this is a Foden FG dumper truck. Gardner diesels or Foden two-stroke diesels could be specified. The heavy-duty chassis provides a front towing eye in the event of difficulties.

Peter Thompson is a well-known lorry preservationist and his latest restoration is this short wheelbase Bedford D Type, a development of the A Type. It has a Perkins diesel engine and embodies the normal control Bedford, developing into the TJ type, which was still being made at the end of Bedford production in the 1980s.

Commers were another mass-produced type, made by the Rootes Group. The Q Type, seen here, was a new concept in the late 1940s with an underfloor engine. A new revolutionary three-cylinder, two-stroke diesel was later fitted to the Q Types, giving out a very distinctive exhaust note.

Is a skip lorry a tipper? Very much so, in order to discharge the skips. The hydraulic lifting gear and the chains, suitably configured, see to the tipping of the load. This is a handsome ERF KV, not usually seen as a skip lorry.

A means of increasing payload capacity was to have a third-axle conversion carried out. This Dodge D700 is a comparative lightweight lorry, on eight stud wheels, and the twin steer conversion would allow around a 3-ton increase in the payload.

A 7-ton lorry, such as this Commer, with a third-axle conversion at the rear was more frequently seen. Usually the chassis went to a specialist aftermarket converter for this work, but Commer, in conjunction with Unipower, listed the type as an option. (Gyles Carpenter)

Bedford had the marketing slogan 'You see them everywhere'. This was certainly the case with the TK model, which was new in 1960. This is a very early model on the erstwhile fleet of Russell of Bathgate. It has 'greedy' or 'hungry' boards fitted to increase the load capacity depending on the density of the load.

Ford introduced the Thames Trader in the late 1950s, covering a wide range from lightweights up to 7-ton capacity. Cab access was never a redeeming feature, but they were put to many uses. The loaded steel tipper body is typical of the time, as is the practise of the work crew being carried among the load.

This is an Albion Reiver with a Homalloy coach-built cab. The Reiver was a six-wheel development of the Chieftain four-wheeler. Coach-built cabs were still being fitted to Albion chassis at this time. Early Albion Reivers were rated as 10-tonners.

The Dodge Kew normal control range was updated with a new cab style in the 1950s, contemporary with Commers. This is an unusual third-axle conversion on muck shifting work, which would be rather underpowered with a Perkins engine.

Bassets Roadways, still in business, is a long-established Midlands fleet. All types of haulage were carried out in the past, of which tippers contributed a large share. Seen here, when new and unregistered, is a Foden FG eight-wheeler with an S21 cab. Note the axle spacing and the position of the spare wheel. It had a gross weight of 24 tons.

This long wheelbase 1962 Thames Trader Mk II was driven by Eddie Waugh, a long-time lorry enthusiast and modeller. The wooden dropside body would allow the lorry to be used for general haulage. Walter Marchbank is still in business as a tipper operator. (Eddie Waugh)

A. C. Penman is an engineering company today. They would have built the demountable tipping body and the platform body fitted to this long Albion Reiver, making it a versatile lorry in agricultural haulage.

The Thames Trader was often converted to six-wheeler configuration, and this example by the old York Trailer Co. is being put through its paces off-road. Different rear hubs suggest a trailing axle 6×2 arrangement.

The Albion Clydesdale was a 14-ton gross weight four-wheel lorry. Like previous Albions, it was a basic, no frills, easily maintained lorry, with a Leyland Comet engine giving just about adequate power. This is another NCB lorry used on the Ayrshire coalfield.

A long wheelbase farm feed tipper in the long-gone Jas. McKinnon Jnr fleet of lorries and milk tankers, based in Kilmarnock. It is an AEC Marshal, being a six-wheel version of the well-liked AEC Mercury. Fitted with a Park Royal cab, it would be one of the last built before the Ergomatic tilt cabs were introduced.

The last of the bonneted Bedfords was the TJ Type. The cab was similar in dimensions to the original A Type shown elsewhere. Articulated tippers of this size were rare by 1965, when the Bedford was new, and it may have been used internally.

Contemporary with the Bedford TJ, but not as long lived, was the BMC WFK100. Generally used by local authorities and small businesses by the 1960s, most went for export. The concept was kept alive into the 1980s with the export-only bonneted Leyland Landmaster.

A heavyweight tipper of the 1960s. A change in Construction & Use Regulations (C&U Regs) in 1964 put eight-wheelers at a disadvantage with restrictive axle spacing. This Atkinson L1786 would have no more than a maximum 26 tons gross weight, against artics at 32 tons.

The Guy Invincible was a groundbreaking lorry with a part-fibreglass cab and wrap-around windows, dual headlights and other internal accessories not fitted in cars at the time. This 1965 late model, restored and worked by the late John Horner, began life as a concrete mixer and then was a showman's heavy tractor before becoming a tipper.

Another Thames Trader Mk II. These were seen as cheap lorries which were worked hard and often set aside or scrapped after the first owners had had their use of them. This one, restored as a Forestry Commission tipper, is a late model from the year in which they were superseded by the new Ford D Series.

The 1964 change to gross weights for articulated types brought about a need for five axles at 32 tons gross. Foden produced this 6x4 artic unit for Hoveringham Aggregates, and York Trailers the high but low-side tipper trailer. The entire trailer pivoted above its axles when tipped up and a stabiliser can be seen under the chassis.

From 1964 four-wheel lorries were allowed to have a gross weight of 16 tons. All the mass producers uprated to this weight and Commer came out with the Maxiload, an 8-tonner with a flitched chassis and heavier axles. Moreton C. Cullimore had several. The fleet was noted for the use of Charles Dickens names, this one being *Seymour Snuffin*.

Jim Padkin started his business in tipper haulage with an Albion Reiver. He later restored this 1966 example to replicate his first lorry. The Reiver has a Leyland engine, depending on when it was built, and the LAD cab dating back to 1959. Subsequent updates allowed for heavier gross weights and different cabs.

The AEC range received a new design in 1964 to accommodate higher weights and was fitted with the Leyland Ergomatic cab. The North of Scotland Milling Co. was supplied with this AEC Marshal tipper for bulk feed movement, capable of working with the dropsides removed for other agricultural products.

The Scania 80 Series was a lighter range of lorries produced by Scania across a range from 16-ton rigids to 32-ton artics. At 16 tons the chassis was regarded by some as heavy and expensive. William Sim, an Ayrshire public works contractor, used this one for many years. It carried a striking red and light blue livery.

The equivalent Bedford 16-ton chassis was known as the KM. It used the Bedford TK cab, set slightly further ahead of the front axle, and heavier axles to suit the higher gross weight. Previously the heaviest Bedfords had used Leyland engines, and a new Bedford engine was developed for the KM range. This one is seen making dust in a Fife colliery.

The new C&U Regs of the 1960s allowed longer trailers, as well as higher gross weights. BICC, a firm of cable makers, commissioned this Leyland Retriever and tri-axle trailer for 32 tons gross. An interesting feature was the rearmost tank, which could be tipped for discharge.

The Argyle Manufacturing Co. of East Kilbride produced a number of lorries around 1970, which looked very much like contemporary Seddons. This is a model known as a Christina, built as a 16-ton tipper with a Perkins 6.354 engine. Only a few were sold.

Not a tipper in the true sense, this is a cement bulk tanker that relied on the tank being tipped for discharge. The tractor unit is a BMC Mastiff, for 28 tons, with a Perkins V8 diesel and a Guy Big J chassis. One Glasgow tank haulier, James Hemphill, had a third axle fitted to Mastiffs and ran them at 32 tons.

More relaxed axle spacing rules in the early 1970s saw a resurgence of interest in eight-wheel tippers. AEC had the Mammoth Major, which had one of the more powerful engines for that weight. This one, built as a bulk tipper, has greedy boards to increase the capacity. The Ergomatic cab was a good workplace and could be easily accessed from ground level.

Foden was an early producer of the eight-wheel tipper at the new gross weight of 30 tons. This somewhat plain S80 cabbed tipper has a large bulk body that could be used for most commodities, as seen here.

The articulated tipper did not have much of an advantage over the eight-wheelers by the early 1970s. The additional weight of the combination would equalise the payload capability. The late Robert Laidlaw is seen at the wheel of a Seddon 32:4, which was a rare breed in the Reid's Transport fleet.

The Dodge K Series was a popular lorry in the 1960s and 1970s, with a tilt cab, fitted low to the ground and given excellent access and a good all-round view. Originally Cummins V6 and V8 engines were fitted, but the majority had Perkins 6.354 diesels.

A preserved AEC Mercury in an old Amey Roadstone livery. The Mercury was capable of running at 24 tons gross, as an artic unit. That capability was possible with the attached trailer, having a four-in-line wheel arrangement, sometimes known as twin oscillating axles, which was well liked in the 1960s, being lighter in weight with little tyre scrub.

In order to achieve 32 tons gross weight some articulated tippers had five axles. This Foden has an extra steering axle to achieve 32 tons gross. It has a spacious Foden S60 cab, styled on Foden dumper truck cabs of the time. The ribbed bathtub trailer body with no sharp inside angles gave a clean discharge of most materials.

The Gardner-engined ERF 54G was not always the first choice as a tipper, and were fairly rare. This LV-cabbed example, operated by Morriston Transport of Ayrshire, has dropsides and a reasonably long body, making it suitable for other agricultural work. The traditional ERF 'greyhound' chassis is clearly visible.

The ubiquitous Bedford TK reigned for a long time as a medium and lightweight tipper up to and long after Bedford ceased production. This one, possibly a 1260, with a 330 cu. inch Bedford diesel, was on show at Brough during the 2018 Cumbria Easter vintage show.

Atkinson lorries only gradually changed their appearance over the years. This L1786 model has a long bulk tipping body, a long wheelbase and probably a wide turning circle. It is seen at an Atkinson Gathering at the British Commercial Vehicle Museum.

Another less obvious tipping type was the local authority drain cleaner. Designed as vacuum tankers, they required a tipping ability to discharge the collected load. This Karrier 7-tonner, essentially a Commer, was how they were marketed to municipal users, in this case Inverness Town Council.

An AEC Mandator in the fleet of Taymix Transport of Blandford, Dorset. The AEC Mandator had a large AEC engine, among the most powerful of its time. The Tasker trailer, built purely as a bulk type, gives a balanced look to the combination, running at 32 tons gross. Relaxed axle spacing had allowed 32 tons on four axles when the AEC was new.

The insurgence of European lorries was evident in the UK by the early 1970s. Magirus Deutz had entered the UK market with air-cooled engines, usually as artic units. The bonneted Magirus Deutz 232 found favour as a site dumper, with a road legal capability.

In the late 1960s Leyland introduced a new series of lorries known as the 500 Range, with fixed cylinder head engines, supposedly to rationalise and replace former Leyland and AEC types. The model range included six-wheelers known as Bisons. The Ergomatic cab was retained, but the engines were troublesome, giving the range a poor reputation.

The interest in this picture comes from the tipping trailer. It was designed by Neville Charrold in an attempt to increase stability when tipped. The trailer tipped around the rear axle axis, with stabilisers on both sides. The trailer automatically retracted forward to the artic unit when the body was raised.

Another picture of the retracting tipping trailer, in preservation, now badged as being made by the former York Trailers. It could be coupled to any standard four-wheel artic unit.

When Scania entered the UK market they did not make an eight-wheeler type, which was then a rare thing in Sweden. A 6×4 tractor unit was developed, experimentally, with an extra steering axle added and a tipper body fitted. It ran in the Russell of Bathgate fleet before going to Reid's Transport. It was deemed too heavy and no more factory-built Scania eight-wheelers were made for the UK until the 82 and 112 series were announced.

Perhaps not the clearest photo of a tipper, but it shows an early imported Mercedes Benz LP2419 being used as a tipper. The high access cab was probably not the best for tipper work, while the trunnion-mounted rear axles were troublesome.

This late model Albion Clydesdale was registered in 1974, well after the end of the model line. It was operated originally as a farm feed bulk tipper, going into preservation in that condition. A basic lorry, in the Albion tradition, it is now in the hands of Neil Williams, a well-known Edinburgh-based tipper operator.

Taking the Bedford four-wheel tipper range of lorries into the 1964 C&U Regs upgrade to 16 tons was the Bedford KM, characterised by the widened cab wings and the double bumper. This one is seen parked in a Glasgow street when it was fairly new.

Foden had a good reputation for building strong lorries eminently suitable as tippers. This Foden, with an S39 cab, was bought second hand by an Ayrshire operator and is waiting to discharge a load of tarmacadam. The driver is using the waiting time to check his vehicle.

Seddon rationalised their range of lorries in the 1960s, beginning with the 13:4 using a Motor Panels cab, similar to Guy and other makes. The 13:4 evolved to a 16-tonner and this example, in preservation, shows a long wheelbase tipper that could be used for general haulage.

After the A Series, mainly of tractor units, ERF announced the tilt cab B Series in 1975, available as a full range of lorries. The well-known Knowles Transport had this 30-ton gross B Series eight-wheeler for bulk tipper haulage, seen here in the red Knowles livery style.

When Volvo entered the UK market the emphasis was on artic units, with the low cabbed F86 type. It was a resounding success, which led to greater things. Four-wheel Volvo F86 lorries were in the minority, usually as wagon and drag types. Tipper versions were not common. This insulated tipper was parked at Tweedmouth harbour in 2007.

Another Foden tipper, this time sporting an S80 cab, which was designed to be in competition with the then imported European large-cabbed types. In reality the cab was not really very spacious, having a large engine cover, and access through the short and narrow doors was not ideal.

McQuater Bros. was a long-established farm feed merchant in Ayrshire. In the later years of business the fleet was dominated by Ford lorries, and this D Series was one of the last used. It had a multi-compartment body for different quantities of feed, tipping to the rear for pneumatic discharge.

No lorry book should be without a picture from the legendary Brian Harris fleet from Devon. Tippers were in the minority in the Harris fleet, and this ERF B Series shows the versatility of the long wheelbase, giving plenty of body space for general haulage. It carries the original Harris & Miners livery.

The Hillhouse Quarry Co. once had their own fleet of lorries, mainly Fodens, and this S39-cabbed six-wheel tipper was one of a number in use. This model was sometimes known as a 'Sixer', which had a dedicated six-wheel chassis for tippers and concrete mixers.

The Volvo F86 became popular as a six-wheel lorry, and many were used as tippers. Some were 6×2, with lifting rear axles, and others were double drive, according to buyer preferences. Long and short wheelbases were available and this one, in preservation, had folding sides to accommodate general agricultural haulage.

Magirus Deutz did not have as much success as the Volvo and Scania imports, but by the late 1970s a substantial number were running as tippers. Six- and eight-wheelers were available and a 232 bhp engine, which was air-cooled, meant less maintenance. This one, obviously being worked hard, is seen in the pre-sheeting days.

Although a tipper, this ERF B Series shows the versatility of the long body which is being used to accommodate a good load of baled fodder. It was part of a small Devonian fleet, operated by Edwin Cunningham, in the 1980s. (P. Crang)

Another Edwin Cunningham tipper, well laden with rocks for beach defences. Pat Crang, a former driver, says it had had this scow end body for rock haulage and a normal tipper body for tarmac. (P. Crang)

The Scammell Routeman, at 30 tons gross, became a well-respected tipper in the British Leyland line-up. Most had double drive, like this one, which is now in preservation, having first served with an Edinburgh haulage company. The cab was designed in the early 1960s by Michellotti, an Italian car designer, and stood the test of time to the end of production.

This is a one-off in the Reid's Transport fleet, which at the time was dominated by Scanias. The ERF was kept for local work, usually hauling draff, a whisky distillery by-product, to farms. Harry Craig, the driver, kept it in immaculate condition.

Fodens introduced a new range of lorries in 1977, known initially as Truckmaster. This Archer artic tipper is a Fleetmaster and could be fitted with a Cummins or a Rolls-Royce engine. The tyres on front axle of the trailer have a dubious look!

In the 1970s the Albion Reiver became a Leyland and was built at the then BL factory in Bathgate. It was uprated to 24 tons and became, as its predecessors did, a tipper man's ideal lorry. Loanhead Transport was part of the large Scottish W. H. Malcolm company.

The Chrysler Corporation was the owner of Dodge UK, which did not have an eight-wheeler chassis. Spanish Barreiros heavyweights were imported, badged as Dodges, and were ideal as tippers, being strong and heavily built lorries. Due to their weight, not many were sold. This one was being used on internal coal haulage near the end of its life.

Leyland's T45 range included the 16-ton Freighter, which could be had with various wheelbases. George Wisener used this short wheelbase tipper on local road maintenance and general tipper work. He also used it as a transporter for his collection of vintage tractors, hence the ramp at the rear. (A. Syme)

Another example of the prolific Bedford TK. This is a 7.5-tonne gross dropside tipper and was probably the basis of many an LGV driving career.

What might be referred to as a super-dumper, this tractor unit is an adapted version of a Foden FC35, and was capable of a 35-tonne load capacity as a solo dumper. As an articulated outfit it is likely to have had a payload in excess of 60 tons.

The bonneted Scammell S26 range was designed as an export lorry. Many were used on the Falkland Islands to repair damage after the Argentine incursion. The National Coal Board used some in large collieries. This one operated at Killoch Colliery in Ayrshire and was seen on 'day release' at an engineering company for repairs.

The Leyland T45 range included six-wheel lorries with the Freighter cab and several engines of varying power. Ancell Motors used this Constructor 6 as a coal lorry servicing schools and local authority buildings, tipping the load through a pneumatic blower.

The medium weight models in the T45 range were replacements for former BMC designs, such as Lairds and Boxers. This small Freighter tipper, in the livery of the former Strathclyde Regional Council, was used on road maintenance.

W. H. Malcolm is the largest haulage contractor in Scotland, with depots across the UK. This 1984 Volvo F7 is seen in their Kilwinning depot, close by the Irvine Volvo factory, and was one of a large number running on coal haulage in Scotland. Malcolm frequently assisted Volvo in the development of new Volvo lorry designs.

The NCB changed its name to British Coal, as can be seen on this 1984 Leyland Constructor 8, developed from the Scammell Routeman. It had the wide cab of the Roadtrain artic unit, but could also be fitted with the narrow cab from the Freighters.

In the 1970s Commer produced a new range of lorries from 7.5 tonnes upwards, with a common cab and, usually, Perkins engines. It was known as the Commando. Later, the range was badged as Dodge, but was basically to the original design. The cab remained the same throughout production under Renault ownership.

It was unusual to see a tipper lorry with a sleeper cab in the 1980s, particularly on a four-wheeler. This Leyland Freighter had the highest power rating engine at 170 bhp. It has an insulated body for tarmacadam haulage.

Joe Bradley's immaculately restored 1977 Leyland Bison. The Bradley family are quarry masters in Northern Ireland and this lorry was new to them, working on all types of tipper haulage on their own account. It is a regular visitor to the Ayrshire Road Runs.

Yuill & Dodds is a large Scottish tipper operator and has used almost every type of heavy lorry in its time. This high-sided bulk tipper on a MAN eight-wheeler chassis was on show in an early Scottish Truckfest, as indicated by the lack of vehicles. The 2018 Scottish Truckfest had the complete showground filled with exhibits.

Alan Reaper arriving at the start of an Ayrshire Road Run in his beautifully restored Foden S108. This is very much an east of Scotland tipper, with removable dropsides and greedy boards, allowing versatility in a mainly agricultural area, where it was originally based.

During Ford Cargo production, the heavier end of the range was represented by six-wheel chassis powered by Cummins engines. This was the only Cargo to enter the G&D Cunningham fleet, as it was not considered a success. It was alleged to have poor braking performance.

The MAN range of heavy artic units has sustained a good sales turnover since the original imports, but never equal to that of Volvo and Scania. This 16.332 operated by a Geoff Wilson from Penrith looks a tidy motor, although the trailer seems to have seen a lot of use, perhaps on scrap haulage.

Leith's is a quarrying company and civil engineering material supplier, with a large fleet of lorries in the north of Scotland. This Foden 4000 Series was one of their tarmacadam tippers in the 1980s and 1990s and is seen here on the Isle of Skye, waiting to tip its load.

Wullie Carlton and his father, Ian, brought their perfectly restored ERFs to the Biggar Vintage Show in 2018. Both lorries were new to Ian Carlton, with the ERF E10 replacing the B Series, which went into fairground use before restoration. They carry farm feed bulk tipper bodies, which can be discharged by pneumatic blowers.

The lightest lorry in the Leyland T45 range was the Roadrunner, replacing BMC-designed Terriers. It sold very well in the 7.5-tonne bracket, being lighter than most of its competitors. Dennis (Ben) Gunn is seen driving his Roadrunner on an Ayrshire Road Run, with his personal accommodation in the tipper body.

After the amalgamation of Seddon and Atkinson a new range of lorries was announced. The lighter lorries, generally replacing Seddons, were the 200 and 300 ranges. This bulk feed tipper is a later version on a 2.11 chassis, which has been fitted with a pusher axle to increase the gross weight to 23 tons.

When Japanese Hino lorries began to be imported and assembled in Ireland, there was a steady trickle of the FS and FY models into the UK. They were rare in Scotland. This FS was used by a road maintenance company. The hydraulic grab crane was becoming a common sight on utility works tippers by this time.

Another tanker required to be a tipper. Carntyne Transport used this ERF E10 on sugar haulage. It was loaded with the tanker body raised to fill it to capacity. Carntyne Transport, part of the Scottish Russell group of companies, is very much in business today.

Barr Construction was a large civil engineering company in Scotland. Their fleet, mainly of Leyland lorries, was a common sight. This Leyland Constructor 6 with a high capacity body was the forerunner of specialist waste disposal vehicles when the company began to operate landfill sites.

Earlier in the book, it was said that ERF four-wheelers were not common as tipper lorries. The same could be said in latter days, and this ERF E6 was a comparatively rare tipper. It had a 6-litre Cummins engine and operated in the south of Scotland, along the Solway coast.

Wilson of Coylton was a well-known company in Ayrshire tipper circles, having been established for many years. Coal haulage was a big factor in the company's business, and towards the end of the company's existence MAN trucks were the preference. The driver is talking to the late George Richmond, who sold the lorries to the company.

Carlisle has always been the scene of major transport activity, going back to the days of the railway companies. That has continued into present times with road transport, with many large and small fleets. H. Dickinson used this Scania 143 with a stepped bathtub tipper trailer for various commodities.

Again not immediately identifiable as a tipper lorry, this Foden 4300 is carrying a cattle float, but it is a tipper with the sides folded in. The livestock float is demountable, leaving the lorry as a platform type. It may well be capable of pulling a trailer for fodder haulage.

Some Seddon-Atkinson designs covered the former Atkinson types, such as six and eight-wheelers. The Strato was such a lorry, and this six-wheel tipper was a special low specification model to suit tipper work. It has a normal aggregate tipping body to haul sand and gravel to the company concrete batching plants.

Jas. McKinnon Jnr operated farm feed lorries going back to platform lorries with sack loads. Some of their later bulk feed tippers were Leyland Constructors, two of which are pictured here. The bodies are compartmentalised for batch delivery.

Fitted with wide single tyres on the front axles for better weight distribution, this ERF EC 14 seemed, when new, to have a tremendous power of 500 bhp, at a time when most eight-wheelers had around 300 bhp. It is an eye-catching truck with a stylish unpainted alloy tipper body.

Wagon and drag tipper outfits are possible, but not in this combination. The MAN pulls the trailer to a site and then would work alone while the trailer would be used by the artic unit, which carried a scraper to the site on a low loader.

Brand new and about to be delivered to the new owner, Burnthills Demolition, this Renault G290 was in the forecourt of Gateside Commercials, the Dumfries Renault and Dodge dealership. The body has a high rear crossbar and barn-type doors to allow large pieces of demolished material to be discharged without jamming.

Many of the tipper lorries seen in this book have been farm feed bulkers, and this ERF E8 is no exception. The EC8 is a 265 bhp lorry with the lower-powered Cummins engine option. D. M. Clarkson is in business today, running a mixture of tippers and general haulage lorries.

Operating from Garstang in Lancashire, J. & M. Collinson is a long-time tipper haulier. At the time of the photograph, taken in an M6 service station, this Seddon-Atkinson Strato was one of the newest of a long line of Atkinson eight-wheelers in the fleet. The load is uncertain, but well sheeted.

The Hino eight-wheel tipper was the FY Type, well favoured in Ireland but less so in the UK. The Annandale Coal Co. (ACC) had this one for general tipper work and it was probably used in the construction of parts of the present-day M74.

The island of Jersey has restrictive weight and width limits, resulting in some specialised vehicles. This Bedford, with a TK cab and TL parts, has been greatly modified with a pusher axle, to spread weight, and a driven front axle. To meet the various uses it would be put to, a hydraulic crane is also fitted.

In the present day T. French & Son run an all-Volvo tipper fleet on long distance and local haulage. In the 1990s they used this Mercedes Benz 3229 on coal delivery to schools and council buildings. As shown, it has pneumatic blower delivery.

The Ford Cargo was a good medium weight lorry, this one being rated about 14 tons gross. Fitted with an Atlas crane and a dropside tipper body, Jack Muir most likely used it on local utility contract work where the crane would be an asset.

The Leyland Motors 100th anniversary was celebrated with a display of all types of Leyland lorries in Leyland town centre. This Leyland Constructor 8, in pristine condition, was part of the celebration. It's an unusual name for a plant hire company.

A local authority hook loader and tipper in use by Nithsdale District Council, in Dumfriesshire. This is an ERF EC11, which would have plenty of power on hand for Eddie Waugh, the driver, who kept it in great order considering the conditions he worked in. (Eddie Waugh)

An early Volvo FH12 overnighting in the BP truckstop at Carlisle. The trailer has the now almost universal mechanical sheeting gear, which gives a neat appearance to the outfit. Health and safety equipment is evident on the trailer front to prevent the driver from falling off while using the sheeting gear.

Harbro Farm Sales Ltd is a north of Scotland company that set up a base in the largely agricultural Dumfries and Galloway area. Among the lorries based in Castle Douglas was this Foden 3325. It was essentially the same as the 400 Series, but with a small cab, supposedly making for easier access to farms. Drivers did not like the cab.

The Scania 112 and 113 ranges became popular with tipper operators after the introduction of eight-wheelers. Good engine, gearbox and suspension options paved the way for many sales. Jim Padkin had several in his pleasing burgundy and blue style, making good use of the linear design of the cabs to set out his name and business.

A very high set Renault Maxter, with wide single front tyres. It has a conventional tipping body suitable for any bulk loads. Charlie Lauder runs his smart fleet from Dumfries and is a regular exhibitor in Truckfests.

Another ERF bulk feed tipper, this is an ES8 using the smaller Steyr cab, which ERF used before their takeover by MAN, who were the owners of Steyr. A lifting third axle has been fitted as a means of reducing tyre scrub and damage to farmyard surfaces. (P. Crang)

Foden's 3000 Series was a similar six-wheel tipper to the ERF ES8, with a narrow cab. Andrew Cook put this 3275 model, with an insulated tipper body, into service soon after the 1996 Scottish Truckfest, where it had been shown by the local Foden dealership.

At the 1997 Scottish Truckfest the Edinburgh Foden dealership displayed this Foden 3340 with a high-sided alloy bulk tipper. R. Houston & Sons run a medium-sized tipper fleet from Leven in Fife.

The Volvo FL7 was another popular six- and eight-wheel tipper. R. & A. Muir is a long-established tipper contractor running quarry material and tarmacadam in Ayrshire. This is the last Volvo FL7 in the fleet, restored to as-new working condition.

W. H. Malcolm was a prolific user of the Volvo FL Series and this one was seen passing through Kincardine-on-Forth, where it had discharged a load of coal at Longannet Power Station. The stepped bathtub trailer has a manually rolled top sheet and a health and safety-inspired platform for the driver to work on. (Brian McGinlay)

The next generation of Volvo tippers was based mainly on the FM Series, still using a low cab for easy access. The Bartlett family of Coventry are well known for their immaculately kept fleet, and this dual-purpose tipper epitomises the care and maintenance afforded to their vehicles.

After the closure of Bedford lorry production, David J. Brown restarted lorry making under the AWD name. Brown was already making off-road equipment and adapted AWD types so that the trailers could have driven and steered axles. Drive was taken from the unit rear axle and steering was controlled from the fifth wheel, making the trailer follow the unit with minimal cut in. It was known as the Multidrive system.

Any artic unit could be adapted by Multidrive and this Scammell S26 was probably the sole example of its type. Not many were sold overall. Driving such an outfit was an interesting experience.

The Volvo FM cab was considered too low for some users, and a raised version was produced. That entailed the headlamps being fitted in the bumper and a second step up to the cab floor.

Foden was awarded an order from the British Army for a number of 6x6 tipper/dump trucks. They were fitted with the DAF-designed Alpha cab, a Cummins 380 bhp engine and SISU axles, for a design gross weight of 35 tons. This one, with extended body sides, was used as an internal quarry dumper after Army service.

One of two new tipping trailers on their way to James Smith of Denny, in central Scotland. It is a traditional box tipper on a basic semi-trailer chassis. In combination with the ERF EC14, the outfit would run at a gross weight of 38 tonnes.

When 44 tons became the standard articulated gross weight, six axles were required. The larger-cabbed Volvo FH12 provided such a vehicle, with either tag axles or pusher axles. The Duncan Plant Hire combination is a good example.

Sometimes a large six-axle artic tipper was not suitable for small loads. The Jack-a-box demountable tipper body was developed to fit artic units, turning them into short tippers with a respectable load. This was very useful in tight places, and at least one livestock remover has a short cattle float for that reason.

In recent years there has been a growing desire, particularly in London, to develop 'safety' lorries due to the number of accidents involving cyclists. Mercedes Benz adapted their refuse collector range using a low level cab and long door windows to allow the driver better visibility. This one has a rear steering tag axle allowing 32 tons gross. (Mercedes Benz publicity)

NWH, or Neil Williams Haulage, is a large tipper operator in Edinburgh, having been in business over fifty years. A varied fleet has been operated, with Volvos and MAN types dominating in the present day. This MAN eight-wheeler is seen near the Scottish government offices on Regent Road during the demolition of the St James Centre.

One of the Volvo tippers in the NWH fleet, this Volvo FMX is seen coming out of Leith Street, in Edinburgh, where demolition and rebuilding work was in progress just behind the double-deck Lothian Transport bus.

A Volvo FH12 of T. French & Son is seen travelling along the busy A66 between the A1 and the M6. Flush-sided tipper trailers were considered more aerodynamic for long distance work.

The Hino 700 series of eight-wheel chassis arrived at about the same time as Foden lorry production ceased. The Hino was perceived as a good successor to the Fodens and enjoyed a sales boom in the late 2000s. A ruggedly built lorry, with a Hino 13-litre 410 bhp diesel, they seemed a competent 32-ton tipper, but after the initial sales boom, the type seems to have faded away.

There is always a need for small tipper lorries and the tarmacadam division of Malcolm Construction uses this Volvo FL for small loads and easier access. The front-mounted tipping ram and the dropsides, giving less rigidity, have created a slight bow in the middle of the body.

The IVECO Stralis is considered by some to not be in the same league as Scanias and Volvos, but nevertheless they are a common sight on UK roads. This high cab Stralis bears a Scottish registration, but has its base in west Wales. It is pulling a moving floor bulk trailer for tipping wood chip and other less dense loads.

Moyle Transport runs from Northern Ireland in this attractive style. Their Volvo FH12 44-tonner was running unladen on the A77 one wet and dull day.

Another tipper on a rainy day. Hanson is well known in the UK and other countries, with most of their haulage being done by franchised sub-contractors. This Scania 114, run by A. J. P. Smith, is probably carrying tarmacadam but the weather is not good for the job.

On display at a Scottish truckshow is one of Albert Fyffe's Volvo FM eight-wheelers. It is finished in the traditional Scottish style of green over red, with detailed sign writing and the ubiquitous tartan band. The large bulk body has pneumatic discharge when required.

Seen at the east end of Edinburgh's Princes Street, this very clean Scania P270 has a modern-style livery is and well equipped with spotlights. The dropside tipper body and the hydraulic crane gives the lorry all-round versatility.

The six-wheel tipper at 26 tons gross has become less common in recent times, against an upsurge in 32-ton eight-wheelers. K. Little of Penrith used this DAF 75CF, keeping it in immaculate order. It was taking part in a small truckshow in Penrith.

Iain Watt & Son operates a medium-sized tipper fleet from New Cumnock in Ayrshire, generally with eight-wheelers and artics. One of their insulated tippers, an IVECO Trakker mainly used on tarmacadam haulage is seen in the operating base.

A lightweight MAN TG-L 10.180 lorry in the Edinburgh Council fleet. It has a demountable tipper body, which can be swapped for a gritting body and can also be fitted with a snowplough.

Eddie Stobart had tipper lorries on the fleet some years ago. Walking floor trailers are now favoured for 'wood waste' haulage, otherwise known as sawdust and wood chip. This is a safer method of discharge than tipping up a long, high trailer. A new lighter green 'environmentally friendly' livery is applied to the wood haulage lorries.

Tipper lorries and drawbar trailers are not a common sight. This Volvo FM went on the road on 1 August 2018 with a matching trailer. Although an eight-wheeler with a three-axle trailer, its maximum gross weight is 44 tons. The Volvo, running without the trailer, will gross at 32 tons. (Ian Lawson)

In recent times eight-wheeler tippers have been specified with three axles at the rear, known as tridems. This Renault Range C has such an axle set-up with the rear axle steering, which is retractable when empty, making the lorry handle like a six-wheeler, reducing tyre scrub and surface damage.

Due to the requirement for safer lorries in London, the old established Dennis company has turned to producing such a vehicle. It is based on their refuse collection chassis, with a pusher tridem rear axle set up. S. Walsh & Sons Ltd have ten of these Dennis lorries in operation in London. (Robert Matthews)